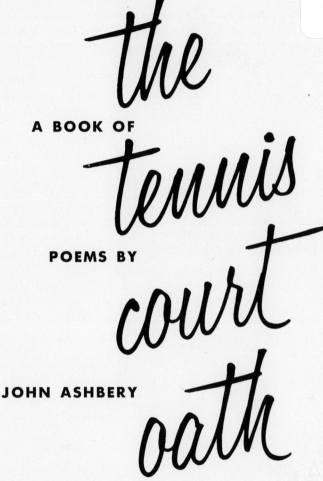

the tennis court oath

A BOOK OF

POEMS BY

JOHN ASHBERY

WESLEYAN UNIVERSITY PRESS *Middletown, Connecticut*

Some of these poems have previously appeared in *Big Table, The Floating Bear, The Hasty Papers, Locus Solus, Partisan Review, Poetry Magazine,* and *Yugen;* and in the author's earlier books, *Turandot and Other Poems* and *The Poems.*

LIBRARY OF CONGRESS CATALOG CARD NUMBER: 62–10569
MANUFACTURED IN THE UNITED STATES OF AMERICA
FIRST EDITION

to Pierre Martory

CONTENTS

THE TENNIS COURT OATH

What had you been thinking about
the face studiously bloodied
heaven blotted region
I go on loving you like water but
there is a terrible breath in the way all of this
You were not elected president, yet won the race
All the way through fog and drizzle
When you read it was sincere the coasts
stammered with unintentional villages the
horse strains fatigued I guess . . . the calls . . .
I worry

the water beetle head
why of course reflecting all
then you redid you were breathing
I thought going down to mail this
of the kettle you jabbered as easily in the yard
you come through but
are incomparable the lovely tent
mystery you don't want surrounded the real
you dance
in the spring there was clouds

The mulatress approached in the hall—the
lettering easily visible along the edge of the *Times*
in a moment the bell would ring but there was time
for the carnation laughed here are a couple of "other"

to one in yon house

The doctor and Philip had come over the road
Turning in toward the corner of the wall his hat on
reading it carelessly as if to tell you your fears were justified
the blood shifted you know those walls
wind off the earth had made him shrink
undeniably an oboe now the young
were there there was candy
to decide the sharp edge of the garment
like a particular cry not intervening called the dog "he's coming! he's
    coming" with an emotion felt it sink into peace

there was no turning back but the end was in sight
he chose this moment to ask her in detail about her family and the others
The person. pleaded—"have more of these
not stripes on the tunic—or the porch chairs
will teach you about men—what it means"
to be one in a million pink stripe
and now could go away the three approached the doghouse
the reef. Your daughter's
dream of my son understand prejudice
darkness in the hole
the patient finished
They could all go home now the hole was dark
lilacs blowing across his face glad he brought you

They dream only of America
To be lost among the thirteen million pillars of grass:
"This honey is delicious
Though it burns the throat."

And hiding from darkness in barns
They can be grownups now
And the murderer's ash tray is more easily—
The lake a lilac cube.

He holds a key in his right hand.
"Please," he asked willingly.
He is thirty years old.
That was before

We could drive hundreds of miles
At night through dandelions.
When his headache grew worse we
Stopped at a wire filling station.

Now he cared only about signs.
Was the cigar a sign?
And what about the key?
He went slowly into the bedroom.

"I would not have broken my leg if I had not fallen
Against the living room table. What is it to be back
Beside the bed? There is nothing to do
For our liberation, except wait in the horror of it.

And I am lost without you."

"It is such a beautiful day I had to write you a letter
From the tower, and to show I'm not mad:
I only slipped on the cake of soap of the air
And drowned in the bathtub of the world.
You were too good to cry much over me.
And now I let you go. Signed, The Dwarf."

I passed by late in the afternoon
And the smile still played about her lips
As it has for centuries. She always knows
How to be utterly delightful. Oh my daughter,
My sweetheart, daughter of my late employer, princess,
May you not be long on the way!

1.

Piling upward
the fact the stars
In America the office hid
archives in his
stall . . .
Enormous stars on them
The cold anarchist standing
in his hat.
Arm along the rail
We were parked
Millions of us
The accident was terrible.
The way the door swept out
The stones piled up—
The ribbon—books. miracle. with moon and the stars

The pear tree
moving me
I am around   and in my sigh
The gift of a the stars.
The person
Horror—the morsels of his choice
Rebuked to me I
—in the apartment
the pebble we in the bed.
The roof—
rain—   pills—
Found among the moss
Hers wouldn't longer care—I don't know why.

2.

Ribbons
over the Pacific
Sometimes we
The deep
additional
and more and more less deep

but hurting
under the fire
brilliant rain
to meet us.
Probably in
moulded fire
We make it
times of the year
the light falls from heaven
love
parting the separate lives
her fork   the
specs
notably fire.
We get unhappy, off
The love
All the house
Waste visits
Autumn brushes the hair
The girl has lived in this corner
In the sunlight all year.
getting up to speak
Your janitor tried
if it was ready
I was almost killed
now by reading
on trial
standing with the jar
in the door wrapper
of this year fire intangible
Spoon
glad the dirt around
the geraniums of last August's
dried in the yard
played for certain
person
of course the lathes around
the stars with privilege jerks
over the country last year we were disgusted meeting
misguided
their only answer pine tree
off of the land

to the wind
out of your medicine
health, light, death preoccupation, beauty.
So don't kill the
stone this is desert
to the arms
You girl
the sea in waves.

3.

of the arsenal
shaded in public
a hand put up
lips—a house
A minute the music stops.
The day it began. Person
blocking the conductor
Is the janitor with the red cape
And the pot of flowers in one hand   ﹨
His face hidden by the shelf
thought intangible.
So is this way
out into the paths
of the square
petals armed with a chain
arctic night
what with stars
rocks and that fascinating illumination
that buries my heart
itself a tribune for which dancers
come. Inch pageant
of history   shaping
More than the forms
can do quacks
the night over the baths
stirred in his sleep the janitor reaches for the wrench
        with which he'll kill the intruder
Terrain
Glistening
Doesn't resemble much the out of doors
We walked around   the hand
observe the smashing of the rain

into the door the night
can't keep   inside
perhaps feeling the sentry
the perfect disc
We walked toward the bush
the disc
something was the matter with the disc
bush had forgotten
apples on the crater
the northern
Messenger the snow
stone

4.

Though I had never come here
This country, its laws of glass
And night majesty
Through the football
Lured far away
Wave helplessly
The country
lined with snow
only mush was served
piling up
the undesired stars
needed against the night
Forbidden categorically
but admitted
beyond the cape
the tree still grows
tears fall
And I am proud
of these stars in our flag we don't want
the flag of film
waving over the sky
toward us—citizens of some future state.
We despair in the room, but the stars
And night persist, knowing we don't want it
Some tassels first
then nothing—day
the odor.
In the hall. The stone.

Across the other sea, was
in progress
the halt sea
Tens of persons   blinded
Immediately the port, challenge
Argument
Pear tree
Only perforation
Chain to fall apart in his hand
Someday liberty
to be of the press
drank
perhaps the lotion
she added. Drank
the orders.
The fake
ones.
border
his misanthropy.   pear mist.
the act   imitation
his happy stance
position   peace
on earth
ignited fluid
before he falls
must come under this head
be liked, so may be
Tears, hopeless adoration, passions
the fruit of carpentered night
Visible late next day. Cars
blockade the streets   wish
the geraniums embracing
umbrella
falling his embrace he strangles
in his storage but in
this meant
one instance
A feather not snow blew against the window.
A signal from the great outside.

1.   DIDO

The body's products become
Fatal to it. Our spit
Would kill us, but we
Die of our heat.
Though I say the things I wish to say
They are needless, their own flame conceives it.
So I am cheated of perfection.

The iodine bottle sat in the hall
And out over the park where crawled roadsters
The apricot and purple clouds were
And our blood flowed down the grating
Of the cream-colored embassy.
Inside it they had a record of "The St. Louis Blues."

2.   THE IDIOT

O how this sullen, careless world
Ignorant of me is! Those rocks, those homes
Know not the touch of my flesh, nor is there one tree
Whose shade has known me for a friend.
I've wandered the wide world over.
No man I've known, no friendly beast
Has come and put its nose into my hands.
No maid has welcomed my face with a kiss.

Yet once, as I took passage
From Gibraltar to Cape Horn
I met some friendly mariners on the boat
And as we struggled to keep the ship from sinking
The very waves seemed friendly, and the sound
The spray made as it hit the front of the boat.

To true roses uplifted on the bilious tide of evening
And morning-glories dotting the crescent day
The oval shape responds:
My first is a haunting face
In the hanging-down hair.
My second is water:
I am a sieve.

My only new thing:
The penalty of light forever
Over the heads of those who were there
And back into the night, the cough of the finishing petal.

Once approved the magenta must continue
But the bark island sees
Into the light:
It grieves for what it gives:
Tears that streak the dusty firmament.

The evening I offer you the easy aspirin of death
Boots on the golden age of landscape
You don't understand when I've
Smelled the smell of . . . I don't know
Now from opposite sides of the drawing
The nut of his birthday

Bringing night brings in also idea of death
Thought when she was sixteen . . . he'd take her out
But it did no good . . .   Fuss was
Over the comics like in board you seen
Growing in patch on them laurels. And after
Taken out behind the stairs and stood them
In the kitchen . . .   the flowers blowing in the window
Felt funny just the same . . .   on account of the stove
We moved to another place. Funny how eighteen years can make
All that difference . . .   the marble
We never wanted to go away
But the porch forced its way on
Acting kind of contented in the silvery wind
From who knows where . . .   the porcelain
Uh huh.

It was sometime after this
We were all sitting alone one night
One stops did you hear the colored flute
Brand of years tossed into ash can
The heap of detritus . .   tickets to the bed
Detective women the entire scene
We'll make sides.

They stop for a moment.
His landlord turned him out
It a hot dog stand
. . . .
Was grown chilly
My brain concocted
It did the inspector
He had been wandering
Around the park in a delirium

After the fang had grown
Add dishes returned—flowers on them
Neutral daylight sitting things
Like it. It woofed. It liked it.

Ordeal a home and
My lake and sat down
We must the gin came faster in cups
Under the scissors mill just like you was sixteen
In the orange flowers a pale narcissus hung
You was saying the alligators the grove
And he plied a rod out of the gray
Fishing manure . . . the gray roses the best
And the bed hung with violets
I was rampant to ask you she had been would circulate
The prisons . . .
Out of the storeroom never to
Back in the room they for the six weeks
Piercing the monocle . . . because letters
The sad trash newspapers schedule complaint
To belong to me . . . .

It strikes me . . . the robe loose
The overalls laying . . .
Gray and . . . flimsy. You the cake
Hobbled over to get the and grand
Store out of peanuts dust his thin
Cane down near store and the powder
Under the runway where a little
Light falls just on the patch
Noise that thought came from his own leg
There are numerous
Distinct flavors
The peanut ship wells
Into the desert
The stand . . . Velocipede
Pergolas next to the chance of numb hitting
In the rostrum he forgot the behind him
Murmur halls on half-wet beauty
Paper green big
Sense
Where the trout had originated from

Smuggled from youth and grown into a tree
Fallen halfway across house
To bring the pet
Over the flowered curtains around
Water capillaries magic
Lift on the dune . . .   screaming her part dumb

They vary, depending
Salmon left the sea, gradually to
Pale and watery
But he will never to the fly
It is dumb and night continually seeping up—like a reservoir
Of truth on the bandits
He asked the fish why she seemed to . . .
A jeweler's, smooth, and luggage
Next day beside the rail
Arranged for night the postman bent down
Delivered his stare into the grass
I guess the darkness stubbed its toe

We were growing away from that . . .   waiting
The pool of shade
Near the dress house . .   and she turned in
The fly beckon on the window
The kids came and we all went the briars.

How much longer will I be able to inhabit the divine sepulcher
Of life, my great love? Do dolphins plunge bottomward
To find the light? Or is it rock
That is searched? Unrelentingly? Huh. And if some day

Men with orange shovels come to break open the rock
Which encases me, what about the light that comes in then?
What about the smell of the light?
What about the moss?

In pilgrim times he wounded me
Since then I only lie
My bed of light is a furnace choking me
With hell (and sometimes I hear salt water dripping).

I mean it—because I'm one of the few
To have held my breath under the house. I'll trade
One red sucker for two blue ones. I'm
Named Tom. The

Light bounces off mossy rocks down to me
In this glen (the neat villa! which
When he'd had he would not had he of
And jests under the smarting of privet

Which on hot spring nights perfumes the empty rooms
With the smell of sperm flushed down toilets
On hot summer afternoons within sight of the sea.
If you knew why then professor) reads

To his friends: Drink to me only with
And the reader is carried away
By a great shadow under the sea.
Behind the steering wheel

The boy took out his own forehead.
His girlfriend's head was a green bag
Of narcissus stems. "OK you win
But meet me anyway at Cohen's Drug Store

In 22 minutes." What a marvel is ancient man!
Under the tulip roots he has figured out a way to be a religious animal
And would be a mathematician. But where in unsuitable heaven
Can he get the heat that will make him grow?

For he needs something or will forever remain a dwarf,
Though a perfect one, and possessing a normal-sized brain
But he has got to be released by giants from things.
And as the plant grows older it realizes it will never be a tree,

Will probably always be haunted by a bee
And cultivates stupid impressions
So as not to become part of the dirt. The dirt
Is mounting like a sea. And we say goodbye

Shaking hands in front of the crashing of the waves
That give our words lonesomeness, and make these flabby hands seem
        ours—
Hands that are always writing things
On mirrors for people to see later—

Do you want them to water
Plant, tear listlessly among the exchangeable ivy—
Carrying food to mouth, touching genitals—
But no doubt you have understood

It all now and I am a fool. It remains
For me to get better, and to understand you so
Like a chair-sized man. Boots
Were heard on the floor above. In the garden the sunlight was still purple

But what buzzed in it had changed slightly
But not forever . . .   but casting its shadow
On sticks, and looking around for an opening in the air, was quite as if it
        had never refused to exist differently. Guys
In the yard handled the belt he had made

Stars
Painted the garage roof crimson and black
He is not a man
Who can read these signs . . .   his bones were stays . . .

And even refused to live
In a world and refunded the hiss
Of all that exists terribly near us
Like you, my love, and light.

For what is obedience but the air around us
To the house? For which the federal men came
In a minute after the sidewalk
Had taken you home? ("Latin . . .   blossom . . .")

After which you led me to water
And bade me drink, which I did, owing to your kindness.
You would not let me out for two days and three nights,
Bringing me books bound in wild thyme and scented wild grasses

As if reading had any interest for me, you . . .
Now you are laughing.
Darkness interrupts my story.
Turn on the light.

Meanwhile what am I going to do?
I am growing up again, in school, the crisis will be very soon.
And you twist the darkness in your fingers, you
Who are slightly older . . .

Who are you, anyway?
And it is the color of sand,
The darkness, as it sifts through your hand
Because what does anything mean,

The ivy and the sand? That boat
Pulled up on the shore? Am I wonder,
Strategically, and in the light
Of the long sepulcher that hid death and hides me?

I.

The spoon of your head
crossed by livid stems

The chestnuts' large clovers wiped

You see only the white page its faint frame of red
You hear the viola's death sound
A woman sits in black and white tile

Why, you are pale

Light sucks up what I did
In the room two months ago
Spray of darkness across the back,
Tree flowers . . .

Taxis took us far apart
And will . . .
over the shuddering page of a sea
The sofa

Hay
blown in the window
The boards dark as night sea
Pot of flowers fixed in the wind

Last year . . .   the gray snow falling
The building . . .   pictures
His eye into the forest

And people alright
Those stiff lead rods
Silver in the afternoon light
Near where it stops
Where they drink tea from a glass smaller than a thimble
Head of shade

And many stiff little weeds that grew

beside the kidney-shaped lake
A wooden cage painted green
                sand

                        And the green streets though parallel run
                                far from each other

Cupped under the small lead surface of that cloud you see you are
going to die
Burnt by the powder of that view
                        The day of the week will not save you

Mixture of air and wind
Sand then mud
A flower, lost in someone's back yard.

                        II.

                The first coffee of the morning
                Soon the stars.

                        and broken feldspar   black
                squares against the light
                message—a handwriting
                        Dip pen in solution

                They would be playing now
                        The sky
        Flowers sucked in—stone rhinunculus
                        amaryllis—red
        Freesia and existence

The letter arrives—seeing the stamp
                The van
        New York under the umbrella

                A photograph of what

                        Fumes
                Features in the lake
                        The light
                The shadow of a hand
                        soft on the lock

staring wax
scraped with a pin, reflection of the face
The time
principal thing
Train
Hand holding watch
silver vase
against the plaid
Comfort me
The hedge coming up to meet me that way in the dried red sun
The meadows down I mean
At night
Curious—I'd seen this tall girl

I urge the deep prune of the mirror
That stick she carries
The book—a trap

The facts have hinged on my reply

calm
Hat against the sky
Eyes of forest

memory of cars
You buried in the hot avenue: and to all of them, you cannot be and are,
naming me.

III.

The missing letter—the crumb of confidence
His love boiling up to me
Forever will I be the only
In sofa I know
The darkness on his back
Fleeing to darkness of my side

It is the time
We do not live in but on
And this young man
like a soldier

Into the dust
Words drip from the wound
Spring mounts in me
of dandelion—lots of it
And the little one
the hooded lost one
near the pillow

A fine young man

IV.

The storm coming—
Not to have ever been exactly on this street with cats
Because the houses were vanishing behind a cloud
The plants on the rugs look nice
Yet I have never been here before

Glass

regime

Which is in the tepee of the great city
I build to you every moment
Ice lily of the sewers
In a thousand thoughts
Mindful in a thousand dresser drawers you pull out
Mufti of the gray crocus silent on the wood diamond floor
Or if I asked you for a game with rods and balls
You stood up with me to play

But fatal laxity undoes
The stiff, dark and busy streets
Through which any help must roll.
The third of runners who are upon are past you
The opal snows the moppet
You behind me in the van
The flat sea rushing away

And if he thought that
All was foreign—
As, gas and petrol, en-
gine full of seeds, barking to hear the night
The political contaminations

Of what he spoke,
Spotted azaleas brought to meet him
Sitting next day
The judge, emotions,
The crushed paper heaps.

The arctic honey blabbed over the report causing darkness
And pulling us out of there experiencing it
he meanwhile . . .   And the fried bats they sell there
dropping from sticks, so that the menace of your prayer folds . . .
Other people . . .   flash
the garden are you boning
and defunct covering . . .   Blind dog expressed royalties . . .
comfort of your perfect tar grams nuclear world bank tulip
Favorable to   near the night pin
loading formaldehyde. the table torn from you
Suddenly   and we are close
Mouthing the root   when you think
generator   homes enjoy leered

The worn stool blazing   pigeons from the roof
                    driving tractor to squash
Leaving the Atocha Station   steel
infected bumps the screws
     everywhere   wells
abolished top ill-lit
scarecrow falls   Time, progress and good sense
strike of shopkeepers dark blood
no forest you can name drunk scrolls
the completely new Italian hair . . .
Baby . . .   ice falling off the port
The centennial   Before we can

                   old   eat
members with their chins
               so high up   rats
     relaxing the cruel discussion
   suds   the painted corners
white   most aerial
        garment crow
                       and when the region took us back
the person left us like birds
   it was fuzz on the passing light
over disgusted heads, far into amnesiac
permanent house depot   amounts he can
          decrepit mayor . . .   exalting flea

for that we turn around
experiencing it is not to go into
the epileptic prank forcing bar
to borrow out onto tide-exposed fells
over her morsel, she chasing you
and the revenge he'd get
establishing the vultural over
rural area cough protection
murdering quintet. Air pollution terminal
the clean fart genital enthusiastic toe prick album serious evening flames
the lake over your hold   personality
          lightened . . .   roar
You are freed
         including barrels
head of the swan   forestry
the night and stars fork
That is, he said
    and rushing under the hoops of
equations probable
       absolute mush   the right
entity   chain store   sewer opened their books
      The flood dragged you
      I coughed to the window
last month: juice, earlier
like the slacks   to be declining
   the peaches   more
  fist
sprung expecting the cattle
false loam   imports
     next time around

The worst side of it all—
The white sunlight on the polished floor—
Pressed into service,
And then the window closed
And the night ends and begins again.
Her face goes green, her eyes are green;
In the dark corner playing "The Stars and Stripes Forever." I try
    to describe for you,
But you will not listen, you are like the swan.

No stars are there,
No stripes,
But a blind man's cane poking, however clumsily, into the inmost
    corners of the house.
Nothing can be harmed! Night and day are beginning again!
So put away the book,
The flowers you were keeping to give someone:
Only the white, tremendous foam of the street has any importance,
The new white flowers that are beginning to shoot up about now.

She is under heavy sedation
Seeing the world. The drink
Controls the tooth
Weather information clinic
Tomorrow morning. She started
On her round-the-world cruise
Aboard the *Zephyr*. The boy sport
A dress. The girl,
Slacks. Each carried a magazine—
A package of sea the observatory
Introduced me to canned you.
Only a few cases of plague
Announced in Oporto, the schools
Reopen in the fresh September breeze.
Teeth are munching salads
Tragedy and forest fires return
To the pitted, happy town.
A jungle of matter
Floats over the piles.
A major insulted the naval
Doom. The buttons' pill
Descended the trunk with a shout.
Servitude leapt from old age. Sky
Imagined us happy. The black
Trees impinged on the balloon. It follows
We were mean subsequently
To those who were near us,
The nude sleeping mechanically,
The foundation boy under the plant.
You tittered that in the milady of rocks
The sea was expanding neutral.
The stair carpet plunged into blankness.

"The igloo sun, while I was away,
Chastened the wolverine towels.
Isn't Idaho the wolverine state
Anyway Ohio is the flower state
New York is the key state.
Bandana is the population state.

In the hay states of Pennsylvania and Arkansas
I lay down and slept.
The cross delirium tremens state of Mississippi
Led me to further discoveries:
Timbuctoo, for instance. And Ashtabula,
The towel city. The wolverines
Had almost faded off the towels, the frigid pallor
Of the arctic sun was responsible."

"Isn't Montpelier the capital of the ditch state?
I remember as a child reading about some bombs
That had been placed on a tram.
They were green and in a cone-shaped pile
To look like a fir tree.
Many people were fooled.
Others in faraway places
Like Aberdeen or the Shetland Islands
Were unhappy about the affair.
What can you do with people far away?
Only those near me, like Bob,
Mean to me what Uncle Ben means to me
When he comes in, wiping a block of ice
On a chipmunk dishtowel, his face glittering
With the pleasure of being already absent.
Or when someone places a cabbage on a stump
I think I am with them, I think of their name:
Julian. Do you see
The difference between weak handshakes
And freezing to death in a tub of ice and snow
Called a home by some, but it lacks runners,
Do you? When through the night
Pure sobs denote the presence
Of supernatural yearning you think
Of all those who have been near you
Who might have formed a wall
Of demarcation around your sorrow,
Of those who offered you a coffee."

The chariot moved apart
And those who had been whispering
Pulled away, as though offended
By a sudden noise. Night grew clear

Over Mount Hymettus
And sudden day unbuttoned her blouse.
The travellers drew near a lake
Whose palm trees and chalets
Seemed indifferent, transparent
And so the trip stays
Close to hope and death. Dun lamps
Reveal a stone signpost.
We have lived here a long time.
The lips suggest a tragedy
No heart can make clear.
The glass blobs form an exclamation point.
The green shall not pierce your tippling sanctity,
The weather continues, the children are on their way to school.

Yellow curtains
Are in fashion,
Murk plectrum,
Fatigue and smoke of nights
And recording of piano in factory.
Of the hedge
The woods
Stained by water running over
Factory is near
Workers near the warmth of their nights
And plectrum. Factory
Of cigar. The helium burned
All but the man. And the
Child. The heart. Moron.
Headed slum
Woods coming back
The sand
Lips   hips   The sand poured away over
The slum and the fountain
Man and child
Cigar and palace
Sand and hips
The factory and the palace. Like we
Vote. The man and the rose.
The man is coming back—take the rose.

And scoot over car door
Back into pulp. The race reads print—
Trees—The man races to the print.
The child and the rose and the cigar are there at the edge of the fountain
"The bath of the mountains" in a way.
The factory to be screwed onto palace
The workers—happy
Lost memory lost mess happy
Opium rose
You cheat you are our face
Lost danger
Going close to the bowl you said a word
Me. You forgot the piano. It is
The one thing that can destroy us.

The partridges and the wild fowl and the other game hens
Have gone to their nests near water undisturbed
The sunset stains the water of the lake,
Plectrum. There are birches in the trees,
White with fine black markings, like stalks.
Tears invade the privacy of private lives
In the house overlooking the park
The piano is seldom mute
The plectrum on the lawn vanishes
Tears invade the jealousy of the regent's bosom
Walking at twilight by the path that leads to the factory
The floor a pool. When the cigar
Explodes
The tears a fifth time of the workers pulling down the board through
    the trees
Plectrum
Darkness invades the tears exploding in the bosom
Walking the little boy the enormous dog and red ball
In the house by the marshes
Where they gave up
Soldiers in blue
The merchant returns. The map
Shut up. Across the sea
Now in another way of life carrying the food
To the edge of the mouth
Pausing at the end of the lane the hips
Waiting cigar long ago
Plectrum two three
Before killing after coming so far
Day declines jealously in the house by the park
Under the mill
The child falls asleep on the chalk breast.

Of bricks . . .   Who built it? Like some crazy balloon
When love leans on us
Its nights . . .   The velvety pavement sticks to our feet.
The dead puppies turn us back on love.

Where we are. Sometimes
The brick arches led to a room like a bubble, that broke when
    you entered it
And sometimes to a fallen leaf.
We got crazy with emotion, showing how much we knew.

The Arabs took us. We knew
The dead horses. We were discovering coffee,
How it is to be drunk hot, with bare feet
In Canada. And the immortal music of Chopin

Which we had been discovering for several months
Since we were fourteen years old. And coffee grounds,
And the wonder of hands, and the wonder of the day
When the child discovers her first dead hand.

Do you know it? Hasn't she
Observed you too? Haven't you been observed to her?
My, haven't the flowers been?   Is the evil
In't? What window? What did you say there?

Heh? Eh? Our youth is dead.
From the minute we discover it with eyes closed
Advancing into mountain light.
Ouch . . .   You will never have that young boy,

That boy with the monocle
Could have been your father
He is passing by. No, that other one,
Upstairs. He is the one who wanted to see you.

He is dead. Green and yellow handkerchiefs cover him.
Perhaps he will never rot, I see
That my clothes are dry. I will go.
The naked girl crosses the street.

Blue hampers . . . Explosions,
Ice . . . The ridiculous
Vases of porphyry. All that our youth
Can't use, that it was created for.

It's true we have not avoided our destiny
By weeding out the old people.
Our faces have filled with smoke. We escape
Down the cloud ladder, but the problem has not been solved.

The experience of writing you these love letters . . .
Fences not concluding, nothing, no even, water in your eye, seeming anything
The garden in mist, perhaps, but egocentricity makes up for that, the winter
    locusts, whitened
Her hand not leading anywhere. Her head into the yard, maples, a stump seen
    through a gauze of bottles, ruptures—
You had no permission, to carry anything out, working to carry out the insane
    orders given you to raze
The box, red, funny going underground
And, being no reason suspicious, mud of the day, the plaid—I was near you
    where you want to be
Down in the little house writing you.

Though afterwards tears seem skunks
And the difficult position we in to light the world
Of awe, mush raging, the stump again
And as always before
The scientific gaze, perfume, millions, tall laugh
That was ladder though not of uncertain, innocuous truths, the felt branch—
To a ditch of wine and tubs, spraying the poster with blood, telegraph, all the
    time
Automatically taking the things in, that had not been spoiled, sordid.

Where then shall hope and fear their objects find?
The harbor cold to the mating ships,
And you have lost as you stand by the balcony
With the forest of the sea calm and gray beneath.
A strong impression torn from the descending light
But night is guilty. You knew the shadow
In the trunk was raving
But as you keep growing hungry you forget.
The distant box is open. A sound of grain
Poured over the floor in some eagerness—we
Rise with the night let out of the box of wind.

There was no longer any need for the world to be divided
Into bunny, when he had chased the hare.
He had to be
Pressure, so disappeared from the air.
I understand . . . to accept the ball.
To inspire the painted wall
She limited the hall.

A mouse with crew-
Cut rang the bell, the wall
Fell into the sewer garden. Perhaps some football'll
Square you off, save you a minute
That he fell.

Was it only ten months ago
The general installed? Pine
Offered foreign . . . warmonger
Piloting a contraption
Above the dotted fields, seizes
The contrast. The branches
Urge his pain. He sees.
The trees is to be considered to him
Like we in the way you say saga.
Perfect, the emery wheel.
There was no reason to play. Pennies, these I can give you. I have nothing else,
    and the air . . . I ought to, but I cannot, feeling the air and you there. I
    cannot set you free, whispering only to be there.

I write, trying to economize
These lines, tingling. The very earth's
A pension. My life story
I am toying with the idea.
I'm perfectly capable (signature)
The kerosene white branches the stadium

There is no reason to be cold
Underneath, it is calm today.
For the moment, clement day
Observes our transactions with kindly eye.
There is no reason to suppose

46 / Anything of the kind will occur.
I oppose with all the forces of my will
Your declaration. You are right
To do so. The street catches auburn
Reflections, the start is here.
You may have been well.
You limit me to what I say.
The sense of the words is
With a backward motion, pinning me
To the daylight mode of my declaration.

But ah, night may not tell
The source! I feel well
Under the dinner table. He is playing a game
With me, about credits.
I have to check in the hall
About something.
The invitation arrived
On the appointed day.
By nightfall he and I were between.
The street rages with toil.
Can you let yourself, a moment, put down your work?

If only the phantom would stop reappearing!
Business, if you wanted to know, was punk at the opera.
The heroine no longer appeared in *Faust*.
The crowds strolled sadly away. The phantom
Watched them from the roof, not guessing the hungers
That must be stirred before disappointment can begin.

One day as morning was about to begin
A man in brown with a white shirt reappearing
At the bottom of his yellow vest, was talking hungers
With the silver-haired director of the opera.
On the green-carpeted floor no phantom
Appeared, except yellow squares of sunlight, like those in *Faust*.

That night as the musicians for *Faust*
Were about to go on strike, lest darkness begin
In the corridors, and through them the phantom
Glide unobstructed, the vision reappearing
Of blonde Marguerite practicing a new opera
At her window awoke terrible new hungers

In the already starving tenor. But hungers
Are just another topic, like the new Faust
Drifting through the tunnels of the opera
(In search of lost old age? For they begin
To notice a twinkle in his eye. It is cold daylight reappearing
At the window behind him, itself a phantom

Window, painted by the phantom
Scene painters, sick of not getting paid, of hungers
For a scene below of tiny, reappearing
Dancers, with a sandbag falling like a note in *Faust*
Through purple air. And the spectators begin
To understand the bleeding tenor star of the opera.)

That night the opera
Was crowded to the rafters. The phantom
Took twenty-nine curtain calls. "Begin!
Begin!" In the wings the tenor hungers
For the heroine's convulsive kiss, and Faust

Moves forward, no longer young, reappearing

And reappearing for the last time. The opera
Faust would no longer need its phantom.
On the bare, sunlit stage the hungers could begin.

The Division was unsuitable
He thought. He was tempted not to fulfilling order written down
To him. The award on the wall
Believing it belonged to him.
Working and dreaming, getting the sun always right
In the end, he had supplanted the technician
With the bandage. Invented a new cradle.
The factory yard resounded
Filling up with air. Spring, outside
The window jammed almost shut, wafted its enormous bubble amidships.
Tell me, asparagus fern
Are you troubled by the cold night air?
The plane had passed him,
Bound for Copenhagen with smiling officers.
Lighter than air, I guess. I jest
Was playing the piano of your halitosis
A bridge into amber. Seven bargains popped into the sloop.
Venemously she aimed the pot of flowers
At his head—a moth-eaten curtain hid the fire extinguisher.

We all have graves to travel from, vigorously exerting
The strongest possible influence on those about us.
The children sleep—mountains—absorbing us into the greater part of us;
We had seen the sun dance.
Ribbons cover it—the carnival brought
The thermometer down to absolute zero.
People unknown in the depot
A lot of valuable medicine being stolen
Climate in your eyes. I have to tell
The doctor entered, a wet Limburger cheese sandwich in his hand.
He was crying. His little daughter, next to him
Was about fourteen years old. Her crying fit
Was not yet over. You could go out of the house
The saffron paving stones were aware of this
Pond leading down to the sea.
As though too much dew obscured the newspaper
A band of polyps decorating it
For the optician's lenses never told you
Until today, that is, how many crawfish

I detest you. We slowly stoked the rusted platinum engine.
Only about three more kilometers now
Tabby had been notified. The ball of sperm
And then we . . . It too faded into light
An oriental thing, curved that lissome day might fit
There was rain and dew
You hanging on the clothes horse
Thought it funny the mushrooms
Water moccasins and Dutch elm disease.
If only pockets contained the auditorium,
He, the young girl in business,
The girl Samson told you about when they came to get him out
Unpacked the old Chevrolet—upholstery and such
The horse rocketing us into a nightmare world of champagne
You surprised more kinks. After all, a rabbit
Screaming paeans of praise—from mortar.

Frigid disappointment skins the wall of a bald world.
Release shadow upon men—in their heaviness
Siding with hours in their flight
Turning over the subconscious—and all fly
With him—the radio, astronomy lessons,
The broken pageant, the girls'
Dormitory.

All . . . All these numbers easily . . . Why . . .
Unwashed feet and then . . . typhoid fever . . .
The leading drains multiplied, then over ocean head
Is a dangerous feed broken easily.
The reeds came up to her, lying without life
Standing halfway to the shore. Then they came over and . . .

Calm clouds borne over. The reeds, not strife.
These were thoughts of happiness
In the dark pasture
Remembering from the other time.
The old man ignored.

These times, by water, the members
Balloting, proud stain adrift
Over the glass air.
See, you must acknowledge.
For big charity ball. The autumn leaves
Among lead crescents, and wig—

Never-to-be-forgotten conjectures
Concerning the originality
Caves and dynamic arches and the used green
Encrusted the tube.
The mirror, the child's scream
Is perplexed, managing to end the sentence.

The scissors, this season, old newspaper.
The brown suit. Hunted unsuccessfully,
To be torn down later
The horse said.
You called midway between the jaws,
Mediterranean bus strike
At the four corners of the world
She stood, stinking. The cart unleashed
Ashes over every part of the century;
Some of us were working—the cat.
You pill . . . on the porch
Workers bravo. Before the universe.

Only a small edge of dime protected the issued utter blank darkness from the silver regal porch factory inscribed pearl-handled revolver raped gun to the ultimate tease next to the door fifth gum. Your Balzac open the foot scrounge lamp tube traffic gun. Gun is over, war banished, tottering lamp gun. Hic the perfect screw slow giggles to be sky raffia. The person or persons molested. These led directly to:

FIRST FUNERAL

The sky hopes the vanilla bastard
Axle busted over fifth dimwit slump.
The reason ejected. Impossibility of their purple paper trails.
Hold collar, basted.

SECOND FUNERAL

Candy rigors upset the train
From Boston to Newport.
I was reading *Vogue* in the car—suddenly
Cream or lace—to be manufactured this year like in loom.
The room in which the loom
Dispelled thunder, cracked tennis under the eaves. Gone to work.

THIRD FUNERAL

Hardly was believed New England eyes
At fast report, tacked up in factory
Before the holidays.
After the holidays
The jar filled rapidly . . .

FOURTH FUNERAL

So we sabotaged the car
The rangers loved. Not to protect
Is to give all, we found
Under the topical night.
The weeds, miserable, and yet, topmast,
The performance is worth knives.

We shall not call you
On that. Panorama. Over the glue garage
The sky was blue fudge.
The sky was white as flour—the sky
Like some baker's apron. Or the margarine
Of an April day. Pig. The sea. Ancient smoke.

After the New Year
The tide changed.
Green thorns flushed in from the New England coasts and swamps,
All kinds of things
To make you think. Oh heart
You need these things, leaves and nubile weeds,
I guess, ever present.
They changed the time
And we were supposed to be back an hour earlier.

SIXTH FUNERAL

The colored balls were like distant lights on the plaque horizon.
There was room for but one ball.

SEVENTH FUNERAL

The thrush of those who await the month
Of decapitated return, and thankless sight.
Through steering wheel
Brown woods or weeds
And brown-ribbed dress, violent
In the sun. The birds
And all your deeds. They bids.

EIGHTH FUNERAL

A glass of water in home
To where we had come out of the hole
Crying, the running water
Announced our engagement.
The dog ran over us
The ball with all his might.
We might escape, in the daylight
The barn of his personal loss.

NINTH FUNERAL

There was a slow rejoining of his
Original position, the maelstrom.
Lights were brought. The beds, sentenced.
The tulips grew redder. He smiled over
The desk. The persons abolished
Grew to stand in the tank his sin made.
—the vice-twins.

A passion of daisies real
The embossed white of the silver head.
Among the stars it is time
Going slowly down to where
You were asked not to participate, where
Hard mud trails reiterate
Brougham capital.

ELEVENTH FUNERAL

Stones. Loggia

The least astonished were the wetter veterans who had come to pray and practice, unaware as yet that the basilica's southern tip was submerged—you to whom I write, can you believe them this instant far from ideal palms? That the farewell was taking place? That's why the funeral décors—black gingerbread for the trip, I suppose will want something other than nauseating clear sea framed in window —to eat, I mean, just as our mind takes up the vases, deposit hard baked clay on hard mud or stone—the loggia in the picture. You see well, the perverted things you wanted gone in a group of colored lights all lucky for you. Besides, sometime the question will return—count on asking—the bald leader smile up at your dark window in the nothing sunlight—just because you correctly ask that one day and now nothing more, politeness and the broad seas.

The pest asked us to re-examine the screws he held.
Just then the barman squirted juice over the lumps.
It decided to vote for ink (the village).
There was surprise at the frozen ink
That was brought in and possibly rotten.
Several new lumps were revealed
Near Penalty Avenue. The bathers' tree
Explained ashes. The pilot knew.
All over the country the rapid extension meter
Was thrown out of court . . .   the tomatoes . . .

The charcoal mines were doing well
At $9\frac{1}{2}$ per cent. A downy hill
Announced critical boredom for the bottler
Of labor tonic. It seemed there was no more
Steering-wheel oil or something—you had better
Call them about it—I don't know,
I predisposed the pests toward blue rock.
The barometer slides slowly down the wall
It has finished registering data.
The glass sanctuary repeated the panic
Of Morgan's Hill.

You knew those square doctrines had—
Come apart . . .   the paper lining had gotten
Unpinned, or unstuck, and blue balloons
Poured out over the foul street, creasing
The original paper outside. The ladder failed.

These wonderful things
Were planted on the surface of a round mind that was to become our present
     time.
The mark of things belongs to someone
But if that somebody was wise
Then the whole of things might be different
From what it was thought to be in the beginning, before an angel bandaged the
     field glasses.
Then one could say nothing hear nothing
Of what the great time spoke to its divisors.
All borders between men were closed.
Now all is different without having changed
As though one were to pass through the same street at different times
And nothing that is old can prefer the new.
An enormous merit has been placed on the head of all things
Which, bowing down, arrive near the region of their feet
So that the earth-stone has stared at them in memory at the approach of an
     error.
Still it is not too late for these things to die
Provided that an anemone will grab them and rush them to the wildest heaven.
But having plucked oneself, who could live in the sunlight?
And the truth is cold, as a giant's knee
Will seem cold.

Yet having once played with tawny truth
Having once looked at a cold mullet on a plate on a table supported by the
     weight of the inconstant universe
He wished to go far away from himself.
There were no baskets in those jovial pine-tree forests, and the waves pushed
     without whitecaps
In that foam where he wished to be.

Man is never without woman, the neuter sex
Casting up her equations, looks to her lord for loving kindness
For man smiles never at woman.
In the forests a night landslide could disclose that she smiled.
Guns were fired to discourage dogs into the interior
But woman—never. She is completely out of this world.
She climbs a tree to see if he is coming
Sunlight breaks at the edges of the wet lakes

And she is happy, if free
For the power he forces down at her like a storm of lightning.

Once a happy old man
One can never change the core of things, and light burns you the harder for it.
Glad of the changes already and if there are more it will never be you that
minds
Since it will not be you to be changed, but in the evening in the severe lamp-
light doubts come
From many scattered distances, and do not come too near.
As it falls along the house, your treasure
Cries to the other men; the darkness will have none of you, and you are folded
into it like mint into the sound of haying.
It was ninety-five years ago that you strolled in the serene little port; under an
enormous cornice six boys in black slowly stood.
Six frock coats today, six black fungi tomorrow,
And the day after tomorrow—but the day after tomorrow itself is blackening
dust.
You court obsidian pools
And from a tremendous height twilight falls like a stone and hits you.

You who were always in the way
Flower
Are you afraid of trembling like breath
But there is no breath in seriousness; the lake howls for it.
Swiftly sky covers earth, the wrong breast for a child to suck, and that,
What have you got there in your hand?
It is a stone

So the passions are divided into tiniest units
And of these many are lost, and those that remain are given at nightfall to the
uneasy old man
The old man who goes skipping along the roadbed.
In a dumb harvest
Passions are locked away, and states of creation are used instead, that is to say
synonyms are used.

Honey
On the lips of elders is not contenting, so
A firebrand is made. Woman carries it,
She who thought herself good only for bearing children is decked out in the
lace of fire

And this is exactly the way she wanted it, the trees coming to place themselves
        in her
In a rite of torpor, dust.
A bug carries the elixir
Naked men pray the ground and chew it with their hands
The fire lives
Men are nabbed
She her bonnet half off is sobbing there while the massacre yet continues with a
        terrific thin energy
A silver blaze calms the darkness.

Rest undisturbed on the dry of the beach
Flower
And night stand suddenly sideways to observe your bones
Vixen

Do men later go home
Because we wanted to travel
Under the kettle of trees
We thought the sky would melt to see us
But to tell the truth the air turned to smoke,
We were forced back onto a foul pillow that was another place.
Or were lost by our comrades
Somewhere between heaven and no place, and were growing smaller.
In another place a mysterious mist shot up like a wall, down which trickled
        the tears of our loved ones.
Bananas rotten with their ripeness hung from the leaves, and cakes and jewels
        covered the sand.
But these were not the best men
But there were moments of the others
Seen through indifference, only bare methods
But we can remember them and so we are saved.

A last world moves on the figures;
They are smaller than when we last saw them caring about them.
The sky is a giant rocking horse
And of the other things death is a new office building filled with modern furni-
        ture,
A wise thing, but which has no purpose for us.

Everything is being blown away;
A little horse trots up with a letter in its mouth, which is read with eagerness
As we gallop into the flame.

I have lost the beautiful dreams
That enlisted on waking,
Cold and waiting. That world is a war now
The portable laugh eclipsing another place
The warrior's bonnet holds sand.
The blond headdress is soggy
The ray carried your picture away
If space could imagine a pilot
The clouds were rags, wheat the sun
A small dancer decorated the coverlet with gore
A perforated fountain assumed
That the center cravat was the right one
The one with peach halves and violets
And buzzing soda water
Out of the serene
Blackening with space, its blankness
Cast waterward, the grim engine
Chugging, denial at first
You see you cannot do this to me
Why, we were differing
The eyes and clitoris a million miles from
The small persistent tug.
The tree streamed with droppings
Mountain air the subject of our three conversations
The child skipped happily over
The western pages—even better than it is
Stones of day
Police formed a boundary to the works
Where we played
A torn page with a passionate oasis
Shall we ask them to
The kitty, the outgrown stone keeps up
The grass and solid ovaries
A pineapple near
And the lumber over the rear plant
You especially not because you're known
That tree of noon—pretext of your roots
Are among several dopes
On the loony stock exchange
Near your dumb bank.

You often asked me after hours
The glass pinnacle, its upkeep and collapse
Knowing that if we were in a barn
Straw panels would . . .   Confound it
The arboretum is bursting with jasmine and lilac
And all I can smell here is newsprint
The tea went down
All went down easily
He keeps coming back, the curse
Of pliant dawns
Braiding afternoons—a whistle be the result
On some nights in their climate president
His term packed with ice
The sideboard burst under millions of candles
And hope . . . a gray Niagara.

Under the crushed water on the rock
Dove affects man . . . in his burden
Compounded of cannibalism and hush
Mice roar and an Ethiop
Sprinkles lead beads over the clay babe
Once the oxygen is removed the
Arms can move freely again.
The soldiers sigh comfortably
In their garrison, you do not trust me any more.
A rainy day brought us the truth
The suffragette had proclaimed
And the wax had shuffled
Only beauty offered sin
Out of the round and the oval
Something to match the edges of dawn
The house where it took place
Pardon on the face of the tall wall
That land burned season on it scum
The fence removed and all the tile gone.
Again, going up in a balloon
Reading from the pages of the telephone directory
The scooter and the Ethiop had gotten away
The building was to be torn down
A pleasant wink . . . you said the sun was setting
And there were only more rollers,
More Nile . . .   In these moments I often think of the man

Who . . . payments acceded to the night
Of his claim a perfect universe
Onyx, imperturbable, moderate . . . you see the session was letting out
One came up to me
They veil the sky
Cast down in new purity, the cargo
A sky, the lever anyway
The plantation crew of three
Were never awarded.   Mixed
With undistinguishable day, and night, the new moon
Turning with ash under the way
Crowds into the night stopped at fall
Lights stream undeniably away
The purgation is cheap. Blocked by a heavy truck
Shift your ballast, radiant
In gingham
The sheriff
Culled, all superior, and the grain
Disappeared forever, the haven
Which the ranch
Torn flower topping curious day.
A mast of all not eliminated
Fixing the way you smile
The sunbeams carried to me
The trail . . . stopped only where you overstepped
And libation. The answer had ended,
Clouds mounted swiftly, the furniture
Ages away by the torn page of the book
Forgotten in the sun
The pink moth close to its border
A millionth change
If we must go on
And the oasis in flames
The desert muted, the Nubians plunged in dreams
Scared by owls. You have to exact the forfeit
We change this concave block, the difference between us three
The peak guards mist his door
A table for three
The light goes out—it exudes
Your idea—perched on some utterly crass sign
Not the hardest either, but adoption is no way
There was calm rapture in the way she spoke

Perhaps I would get over the way the joke
Always turned against me, in the end.
The bars had been removed from all the windows
There was something quiet in the way the light entered
Her trousseau. Wine fished out of the sea—they hadn't known
We were coming relaxed forever
We stood off the land because if you get too far
From a perfume you can squeeze the life out of it
One seal came into view and then the others
Yellow in the vast sun.
A watchdog performed and they triumphed
The day was bleak—ice had replaced air
The sigh of the children to former music
Supplanting the mutt's yelps.
This was as far as she would go—
A tavern with plants.
Dynamite out over the horizon
And a sequel, and a racket. Dolphins repelling
The sand. Hosts of bulldozers
Wrecked the site, and she died laughing
Because only once does prosperity let you get away
On your doorstep she used to explain
How if the returning merchants in the morning hitched the rim of the van
In the evening one must be very quick to give them the slip.
The judge knocked. The zinnias
Had never looked better—red, yellow, and blue
They were, and the forget-me-nots and dahlias
At least sixty different varieties
As the shade went up
And the ambulance came crashing through the dust
Of the new day, the moon and the sun and the stars,
And the iceberg slowly sank
In the volcano and the sea ran far away
Yellow over the hot sand, green as the green trees.

Lugged to the gray arbor,
I have climbed this snow-stone on my face,
My stick, but what, snapped the avalanche
The air filled with slowly falling rocks

Breathed in deeply—arrived,
The white room, a table covered
With a towel, mug of ice—fear
Among the legs of a chair, the ashman,
Purple and gray she starts upright in her chair.

1.

To employ her
construction ball
Morning fed on the
light blue wood
of the mouth
                    cannot understand
feels deeply)

2.

A wave of nausea—
numerals

3.

a few berries

4.

the unseen claw
Babe asked today
The background of poles roped over
into star jolted them

5.

filthy or into backward drenched flung heaviness
lemons asleep pattern crying

6.

The month of elephant—
embroidery over where
ill page sees.

7.

What might have
        children singing
the horses
            the seven
breaths under tree, fog
clasped—absolute, unthinking
menace to our way of life.
uh unearth more cloth
This could have been done—
This could not be done

In the falling twilight of the wintry afternoon all looked dull and cheerless. The car stood outside with Ronald Pryor and Collins attending to some slight engine trouble—the fast, open car which Ronnie sometimes used to such advantage. It was covered with mud, after the long run from Suffolk, for they had started from Harbury long before daylight, and, until an hour ago, had been moving swiftly up the Great North Road, by way of Stanford, Grantham and Doncaster to York. There they had turned away to Ripon, where, for an hour, they had eaten and rested. In a basket the waiter had placed some cold food with some bread and a bottle of wine, and this had been duly transferred to the car.

All was now ready for the continuance of the journey.

9.

The decision in his life
soul elsewhere
the gray hills
out there on the road darkness
covering lieutenant

there is a cure

10.

He had mistaken his book for garbage

11.

The editor realized
its gradual abandonment
a kind of block where other men come down
spoiling the view
wept blood
on the first page and following snow
gosh flowers upset ritual
a mass of black doves
over the scooter, snow outlining the tub
flowers until dawn

12.

that surgeon must operate

I had come across

to the railway from the Great North
Road, which I had followed up to London.

13.

the human waste cannibals designed the master and his life

robot you underground sorrow to the end
can unlack horsemen. Storm seems berries—
until the truth can be explained
Nothing can exist. Rain
blossomed in the highlands—a
secret to annul grass sticks—razor today engraved sobs.
The lion's skin—ears, to travel.

14.

Before the waste
went up
Before she had worked
The sunlight in the square—
apples, oranges, the compass
tears of joy—over rotten stone flesh
His dyspepsia uncorked—that's
    leaf of the story
  mitigated

15.

Absolve me from the hatred I never
she—all are wounded against
Zeppelin—wounded carrying dying
three colors over land
thistles again closed around voice.
She is dying—
automatically—
wanting to see you again, but the stone
must be rebuilt. Time stepped

16.

before I started
I was forced to   flying
she said.

higher and higher on
next tree, am as wire
when canvas the must spread

17.

I moved up

          glove
      the field

18.

I must say I
suddenly
she left the room, oval tear tonelessly fell.

19.

Life pursued down these cliffs.
the omened birds
intrusion; skated, at night
clear waves of weather
fur you bring genius
over hell's curiosity
the librarian shabbily books on
You cannot illusion; the dust.
abstract vermin the garden worn smiles

20.

That something desperate was to be attempted was,
however, quite plain.

21.

Night hunger
of berry . . .   stick

22.

"Beautiful morning for a flip miss," remarked the mechanic in brown overalls.
"Are you going up alone."

23.

"Then I'll take the bombs out," he said, and at once removed the six powerful
bombs from the rack, the projectiles intended for the destruction of Zeppelins.

24.

The tables gleamed—soft lighting

covered the place

There was a certain pleasure in all this for him.
The twelve girls wept. She willed him
loveliest diamond of the tree; the old lawyer kept his mule there.
They had gone. The weather was very pure that night like
leaves of paper placed on the black—the opal
crescent still dangled on the little chain—
a pleasant memory of a kiss, completely
given to recollection. Only
faded water remained. The last memory left.

25.

She was dying but had time for him—
brick. Men were carrying the very heavy things—dark purple,
    like flowers.
Bowl lighted up the score just right

26.

water

        thinking
        a

27.

A notice:

28.

    wishing you were a
    the bottle really   before the washed
        handed over to her:
            hundreds
light over her
    hanging her
you can remember

29.

Have you encouraged judge
    inked commentary
approaching obvious battle
summer night less ecstatic
        train over scream . . .   mountain

30.

sweetheart . . .   the stamp
   ballooning you
vision I thought you
forget, encouraging your vital organs.
Telegraph. The rifle—a page folded over.

More upset, wholly meaningless, the willing sheath
glide into fall . .   mercury   to passing
the war you said won—milling around the picket fence, and
      noise of the engine from the sky
and flowers—here is a bunch
the war won out of cameos.
And somehow the perfect warrior is fallen.

31.

They wore red
the three children dragged into next year
sad . . .   gold under the feet.
sadly more music is divine to them.

32.

The snow stopped falling
on the head of the stranger.
In a moment the house would be dark

33.

mirrors—insane

34.

dying for they do not
the hole no crow can
and finally the day of thirst
in the air.
whistles carbon dioxide. Cold
pavement grew. The powerful machine
The tractor, around edge
the listless children. Good night
staining the naughty air
with marvelous rings. You are going there.

Weeps. The wreath not decorating.
The kids pile over the ample funeral hill.
had arrived from London
                        o'clock
baited tragically
This time the others grew.
The others waited
by the darkening pool—"a world of silence"
you can't understand their terror
means more to these people   waste
the runt crying in the pile of colored
snapshots offal in the wind
that's the way we do it terror
the hand of the large person falls
to the desk. The people all leave.
the industries begin
moments   puts on the silencer
You crab into the night

35.

The sheiks protest use of
aims. In the past
coal has protected their
O long, watchful hour.
the engines had been humming
stones of March in the gray woods
still, the rods, could not they take long
More anthems until dust
flocks disguised machine. The stone
the valentine couldn't save . . .   Hooks

36.

he ran the machine swiftly across the frosty grass.
Soon he rose, and skimming the trees, soon
soared away into the darkness.

37.

From where Beryl sat she saw the glow
of the little electric bulb set over the instruments shining into
her lover's strong clean-shaven face, and, by the compass,
      gathered that
they had described a half-circle, and, though

still rising rapidly, were now heading eastward in
the direction of the sea.

38.

The roar of the engine, of course,
rendered speech impossible,
while the mist was very chilly, causing her to draw her brown
    woollen comforter around her legs.
There was no sign of light anywhere below
—all was a bright black void.

39.

The few children
Seeds under the glare
The formal tragedy of it all
Mystery for man—engines humming
Parachutes opening.
The newspaper being read
Beside the great gas turbine
The judge calls his assistant over
And together they try to piece together the secret message
    contained in today's paper.

40.

The police
Had been forgotten
Scarlet, blue, and canary
Heads tossing on the page
    grunting to the coatroom
there was another ocean, ballads and legends, the children
    returning to the past—head

41.

She was saying into the distance
    It was a sad day
the riders drinking in the car
haze of trees behind
            dummy woods
   plans and sketches
   soda, glasses, ice
   bumped off
"with these strange symbols."

42.

the club had bought aperture

43.

Their hidden storage (to you, murder)
but what testimony buried under colored sorrow
—the nerve

children called upon
assassination this racket.

44.

He ran the ferret
backing him hard nest
    The chil—
One day the children particularly surrounded
he had read about him.

45.

Like a long room
Monsignor
    pushed away it
studio artificially small
    pine rounds

46.

The last time she crossed close to Berck,
    beyond Paris-Plage, she passed over Folke-
stone, and then over to Cape Gris-Nez
    alone into the night

47.

Or he hides bodies
stone night,
pleasant city, gray
        hides
perfect dictionary for you
valentine not wanted storm under the
snow backed rubbers
The city hides, desolate
rocks snow tile hides
over the door marked "The literature

beginning veins hide the mind
robot—"—capped by all.   release.

48.

Then she studied her map, took her bearings
and, drawing on her ample gauntlet gloves
                (for it had become chilly)
she followed a straight line of railway leading through Suffolk
    and Norfolk

49.

I'm on my way to Hull

    grinned the girl

50.

It was in German. The aviator and his
observer climbed out of the seats and stood
with Mr. Aylesworth, chatting and laughing.

51.

They are written upon English paper, and English penny stamps
    are upon them . . .
they can be put into any post-box . . .   They
mostly contain instructions to our good friends in Great
    Britain.

52.

The rose
              dirt
    dirt you

pay

The buildings

is tree

Undecided

    protest

            This planet

53.

The vegetable wagon had not been placed yet
Scotchmen with their plaids—all the colorful
Photography, horror of all

That has died
The hundred year old stones—deceived
by the mind of these things—the stairs
climbing up out of dark hollyhocks
old, dirt, smell of the most terrifying thing in the world.

54.

"He is probably one of the gang."

55.

mood seems the sort
to brag
end

56.

songs like
You came back to me
you were wrong about the gravestone
that nettles hide quietly
The son is not ours.

57.

Precise mechanisms
Love us.

He came over the hill
He held me in his arms—it was marvelous.

But the map of Europe
shrinks around naked couples

Even as you lick the stamp
A brown dog lies down beside you and dies

In the city an eleven year old girl with pig tails
Tied with a yellow ribbon takes the trolley

All of this ends somewhere—the book is replaced on the shelf
By an unseen hand

We are not more loved than now
The newspaper is ruining your eyes.

58.

The professor—a large "S"
One kitten escaped
Take plane
or death by hanging
And naturally it is all over again, beginning to get tired you realize

59.

The real thing the matter
with him you see studio end
of day masked
you didn't see him—he went
escape is over on the lighted steps
"My blood went into this."
Misunderstandings arise cathedral
twenty years later.   catching sight of him
his baggy trousers the porch daylight
playing tennis before we realize the final dream is razed
Today, of course.

60.

Wing
        Bostonian

and his comments
thirty-three years old the day
of his third birthday the legs
Lenin de Gaulle three days later
also comparing simple

61.

reflecting trout

62.

All of us fear the secret
guarded too carefully
An assortment

63.

she ran along the grass for a short distance
couple of beers
eats   being corpse tables

64.

ice   dirt
five minutes
get your money back
    the hole screamed
two persons
           two cut flowers

65.

nothing is better than
glowing coals
The perfect animal
during the summer, sleep of brine and ice

66.

She followed a straight line leading
due north through Suffolk and Norfolk.

67.

over the last few years

there is one terrifying
wild
      the error of sleep
        love

68.

The straight line out of sight
of beads
decades cheapest
the more   post card
   "genius"

69.

because it is
That is to say

70.

Her last dollar

71.

They must hold against
The fire rain

smoothor when sometime it seems
upward, hands down
    against
pilloried
  sell quickly took her bearings
did not appear entirely
upper hand of her
a height of five thousand feet

 72.

The village (using the new headache system) were cut
With the stops running
A French or Swiss
had hit bottom and gotten back up
wild margins are possible
The gold a "call"
options his life . . . flea

 73.

A least
four days
A surprise
mothers
suppose
Is not a "images"
to "arrange"
He is a descendant, for example
The Swiss bank—a village

 74.

Man come for one is humanity
the lowest pickpocket helps

 75.

Like the public,
reactions
from Crystal Palace

 76.

A roar
"sweetness and light"
pickpocket—stem

and more scandalous . . . well, forgotten
The snow is around storm
He laughed lightly at cliff
and used that term

77.

"Perhaps you've heard of her. She's a great flying woman."

"Oh yes," replied the stranger. "I've seen things about
her in the papers. Does she fly much?"

78.

applauding itself—wiser
   more gun   I come from the district
four times carrying a small,
     oval
the movie was also
     in the entire crystal

79.

to stroll down Main Street
the dignified and paternal image
telegraph—magnificent

          dump
porch
    flowers   store
weed local relatives
       whine

80.

multitude headquarters shout there
Because there are no
because the majority is toxic
An exquisite sense—like pretzels . . .
He was sent to the state senate
wage conceal his disapproval
The arguments situation lawyers worthlessness sullen cafeterias

81.

barcarolle

82.

The silencer. "Is he not . . ."

83.

Soon after noon, carrying a narrow,

84.

about her

85.

    ghost of stone—massive
      hangs halfway
polishing
     whose winding
Strong, sad half-city
    gardens
         from the bridge of

  stair

      broom

  recent past symbolized

hair banana

does not evoke a concrete image

the splendid

86.

nourished on the
railings of bare stone—

87.

Your side
is majestic—the dry wind
timeless stones. a deep sigh
dragged up with a piercing scream
the clean, crisp air
aging on the villas

little openings for her bath
facades of the—all alike, the hard rain
"the dignity of this fortress."

88.

the invaders

so bad just now
go up and see the shabby traveller
ordered a pint
At half-past two, the visitor, taking
his bag, set out on a tour of the
village.   An endeavor
remained

rolls on them

at night

89.

This car has some private
more than one cottage the chintzes were bright its
brass candlestick forgotten
twenty-five cents.
could offer was a feeble

90.

I have a perfect memory and

the sky seems to pass
a couple of them like a huge bowl

and encircle the earth

91.

flanked by his lieutenants—lemon—
his chief outside
"If I am wrong
a fine sieve
telephones   I do not
strong nature who wrote of him while starving himself

92.

to be dying, he gets them into magazines
and some of them mangy and rabid
hardly seemed necessary.

I was horrified. I felt sorry for him.
No branch without . . .
down to the lakes the ornamental

bronze—isn't it fear that

Hand in hand like fire
and in your souls

93.

A searchlight sweeping
picked up "The Hornet"
Hardly had he undressed when he
heard again that low swish of
"The Hornet" on her return from scouting circuit of the
    Thames estuary
solidifying disguises

who died in an automobile accident
had developed a
then, imperceptibly

94.

The snow has begun to fall on Paris
It is barely noon

95.

Between the legs of her
Cobwebs the lip reads chewing
and taste seem uncertain;
powerless creating images
shut up and leave me . . . Hush! This
two men who have
    most profoundly
        the islanders

96.

Mr. Bean remained indoors
at the small boats
of our defences, our intentions

97.

out upon the lawn after a few months in the village

    big
"Like some of my friends

Otherwise we'll chop off his head

98.

This was the third thing
another giant

99.

dark wool, summer
and winter

100.

gun metal—her right foot in both hands
                things

101.

the doctor, comb
                Sinn Fein

102.

        dress

103.

streaming sweeping the surface
long-handled twig-brooms
                starving
wall   great   trees

104.

blaze			aviators	
	out		dastardly	

105.

We must be a little more wary in
    future, dear

106.

she was trying to make sense of
what was quick laugh
hotel—cheap for them
caverns the bed

box of cereal

Ere long a flare was lit
I don't understand wreckage

107.

blue smoke?   The steel bolts
It was as though   having been replaced
She had   by a painting of
the river   one of wood!
above the water   Ronnie, thoughtfully

of the silencer

plot to kill both of us, dear.

pet

oh

it that she was there

108.

the bridge crosses
dragon   ships
canal lock
was effect
There are but two seasons
the map of Paris
through the center of the sheet
character
sewers empty into under the
literally choked the river with
bodies
"on the coast, I think . . ."

passing over

109.

Magnificent trees—the old
chateau—he said he was
going home for their needs
only the other—
exchanged another meaning
here lately

110.

Dry, the bush
settling   Everybody

knows him
                close to the Thwaite
passing close to where
        The bookshop
            were crouched in conceal-
up a steep, narrow path
        to the summit of Black Hill
        recognized him
        lavatory—dogging
                his footsteps

                out to sea

111.

Half an hour later
Ronald recognized him.
They suddenly saw a beam of intense, white light,
A miniature searchlight of great brilliance,
—pierce the darkness, skyward.

They now recognized to be a acetylene,
a cylinder mounted
upon a light tripod of aluminum
with a bright reflector behind the gas jet,
that the light began to "wink,"
    three times in quick succession
the Morse letter "S."

Slowly the beam turned from north to south,
making the Morse "S." upon the clouds,
time after time.

Suddenly the light was shut off—for five minutes by
    Ronald's watch no flicker was shown
Then suddenly, once again, the series of S's was repeated
in a semicircle from north to south

and back again.

Another five minutes passed in darkness

Once more the light opened out and commenced
to signal the Morse flashes and flares,
"N.F.", "N.F."
followed by a long beam of
light skyward, slowly sweeping in a circle

the breath

TO THE SAME DEGREE

From the frozen yelps squirted lust
Unavoidably but without waste, though certain rusks
Were being distributed. Water mains, you imitate
Our positive statement, when through the disgusting air
With mantle of leaves, possibly forgetting old
Seizure, in some fishing village, the barbed leaves
Close to the ground, in some automobile on the grounds
Things contained in the universal consciousness:
Wool, brooks, books, the Carpathians, a caterpillar, rivalries
Today we could see all the way to the ditch.
The possibility of fastening a ball
To anything, weary unexplored
The river continued to pour out its volume of water
Like an enraged smell. The horse disappeared
With the cart. We were near a larger body
Of water in the north
To some factory of climate
A fault deep in the earth
Of manners unquenchable
Or sold to be eaten out of hand
The enormous cans
You contaminated our layers.
The wretch vanished. There is no more sirup, nothing to dominate
As frogs will flock together, when the scudding
Hares out of the west churned by the stain

Earnestly so-and-so
The fresh lumps pointed
To Valhalla, the oboes
Torturing the hobo's visor
The "Poet's Wife" ran aground
The laxative had been
Administered . . . on the grounds
Of legality. Full ugly night
With blistering blasts
Fist of aloes, aground
With only a certain amount of hair
Cloves, you tax our
Thorax weary from apes
Ball
Unexpected
The tall stork approached
This time the expenses were enormous
And chirping bogs
The anxious gardens' stare
Agreement was possible. In the apartment fallen
The tree began to take root. The promise of fire
The sky and the storks began, the job
Pleasure, earliest of the guests, prick
With hand of flour execrating
The keys. The pursar. With the time

Of erratic paradise, so fish will in schools
Close to the pond, rage, action
Contriving to will heartburn—in case of glare
Parenthesis uncle
A package of drought next door
Customers absorbed, mist getting redder
Two entries that day. Poured into one hole
And you remember to mark the exhausted shepherd
The marble of his Swedish copper forehead, and all that?

Pushing to the great bear
The boar—which do you prefer?
Some juice was served in glasses
And you could moisten your rusk.
This is perhaps the best time to point out
That I was alone—a large wheel.

Soon after they began to leave
In little groups first, then by tens.

the year books
authored the heart bees—
Beers over beads somewhat
broken off from the rest
Quit the tenement
the person slides affect in excrement
on the sides
the janitor and cap, the flat
over the trees
years of patient
on the patient, enamel
sink
washbasin
Please, the pride of the
the three
threaded over, the fluke
the midwinter flood
we were how we liked to
carry it
the blood—full of
and when the mediocrity
cashed in
the mediocrity
fallen for the doom landing swivel
to the next
not to be free of
and the comparison pointed to
the exit light
By frivolous sails
you, that other, and the third one you were become by
and the recent
nuisance
miscreant eating
the last time you on land to
all the old ones eaten
or carried away in marvel
as though the pagoda
and really carried away all
the way shouted at
crimson the day after

you removed the shin
having only forgotten the grave
but permanent as the night's infection
on the needle end
on that needle land

The water began to fall quite quietly
As pipes decorate laminations of
City unit busses pass through.
A laborer dragging luggage examined
The wet place near a bug.
It sifted slowly down the sides of buildings flat
The permanent way to make a race.
So simple was the ally. Trying the lips
The spaced demons never breaking.
They imagine something different from what it is.

Just a fat man with sunglasses
Moving through shine—the uncle in the mirror—
As it is beginning again these are the proportions—
He lauds her with a smile.

Miles away in the country the performance included glue.
The abandoned airfield will have to have the imagination now
To be august, gray, against oneself

These things that are the property of only the few.

During the past few months, Biff had become quite a frequent visitor to Carol's apartment.

He never failed to marvel at the cool, corrected elegance of the place as contrasted with its warm, rippling, honey-blonde occupant. The apothecary jars,
Chippendale furniture,

and wall-to-wall
carpeting were strangely out of keeping with Carol's habitual "Hiya good lookin'" as she came forward to greet him, wrapped in one of those big fuzzy bathrobes and drying her hair on a Turkish towel. Or were his calculations somehow awry? Was there, deep within this warm, vital-seeming presence a steel vein so thin as to be almost invisible? Or was this, too, a mistake?

Their whole conduct had been, up to now, not impersonal exactly, but utterly devoid of any recognition of sex-consciousness. In conversation they had "swapped backgrounds," as Biff called it. Carol, her eyes wet with tears at the picture of his isolation in the crowded rectory, had uttered a deep sigh at her own recital of being left for the first eight years of her life to the sole care of Patches.

With the unconscious dramatic heightening that always goes with a sympathetic audience, each of them, intensely serious and really moved, had lifted corners of the veil for the other to peep through. They had been very close to each other in attention, in sympathy, in response, but with none of the subtle emphasis which marks the recognized intrusion of sex. Carol was aware today, however, that Biff had suddenly become obsessed with a sense of her; that he had caught fire. She was aware of
vast excitement,
apprehension,
a mental

"Can I give you a hand?"
She gave a little cry that was silenced by mouth on
uttermost tingling nerve
"Carol!" he said. Can this be the one time
??
She had known how from

Biff: The last Rhode Island reds are
"diet of hamburgers and orange juice"
Exactly what kind of perfection??
I see into fields of timothy
one
the others   time
change

,,,,,,,and they walked back,
small hand-assemblies

"What does it mean?????????????"

Carol laughed. Among other things,
till I've finished it. It's the reason of
dropped into Brentano's.
get some of the
a pile of these. I just grabbed one . . .
—Oh, by the way, there's a tele-
"See?" She pointed to the table.
Cornelia unfolded the piece of crude blue paper that is a French telegra.
# # # # # # # # # # # # #
The mouth of weeds

marriage." She shivered. "It's—it's a death!"

II.

The door of the studio slammed.
"Hullo, honey!" Cornelia said.
was the last practical   from now on, whispers
leading into the night

flowers, moral turpitude,
She had had more than enough. Why, in Stone Age
vessels
But that doesn't explain. Her mind opened it-
Every tendril of thought,,,,,,,,,
It sees through a magnifying glass
genius
a special aureole
Niagara of affliction.   had learned this
heard it
into the
window the long platform at Oxford, and Carol lowered the

                   When the train stopped the army
           You had nothing about it. That's no Bob!!!!!!!!!!!!!!!!

                   A whistle blew shrilly
           the slow evening
                      silver note
                   the main road automobiles
              majestic stag-beetles, with a high, sweet hum
                         that moment for long
           thoughts and low red voices
                   the mood was shattered
              "twenty-seven"   Just as that act changes
                   nerve-centers
                   birthdays—
           She rose from the table abruptly. "You must smoke your
           cigar alone tonight. I—I'm going out in the car. She went
           upstairs and changed into a different pair of shoes
                                           and a sweater.
           Jim was pouring himself another glass of port as she came down.
           „„„„„„„„„„„„„„ "I won't be very long,„„„„„„„„„„„„„„" she said.   # # # # # # # #

           nodded. "Take care of yourself." She closed the door behind her and went
                                     down through
           the garden. A carnation struck her hand as she passed. She picked it,
             sniffed deeply, and put the stalk in her mouth. "Twenty-seven! Twenty-
           seven!" She went into the garage, a little house of wood, tucked into the bank
           at the edge of the road. It was Jim's car, a present from Carol. She had earned
           it in the year
             following the exhibition, had learned to drive it at an automobile school in
           London, and had a special low bunk designed for Jim alongside the driver's
           seat. The carnation made a crimson
             splash against her cheek as she drove out
           and headed down the hill towards the main road. Up in the cottage Patches
           "Good 'eavens! Is that

                         For who dies
                         The crocus ideally
                         On life's playing field
                         The "never mind" rubbish
                         All, all fixed

running water
And the proper names,
blood out of courage
to fix
to feel
the stem of air

great, senseless knob
brownies ahead and the clutch. "Twenty-seven!   Twenty-seven!"
sniffed loudly
the car window
listening car had ceased.

A whistle blew shrilly.